AF255203

MEISTER ECKEHART SPEAKS

MEISTER ECKEHART SPEAKS

*A Collection of the Teachings
of the Famous German Mystic
with an introduction by* OTTO KARRER.

Translated from the German by
ELIZABETH STRAKOSCH

WIPF & STOCK · Eugene, Oregon

Wipf and Stock Publishers
199 W 8th Ave, Suite 3
Eugene, OR 97401

Meister Eckehart Speaks
A Collection of the Teachings of the Famous German Mystic
with an Introduction by Otto Karrer
By Eckhart, Meister and Karrer, Otto
Softcover ISBN-13: 978-1-6667-7714-7
Hardcover ISBN-13: 978-1-6667-7715-4
eBook ISBN-13: 978-1-6667-7716-1
Publication date 4/4/2023
Previously published by Philosophical Library, 1956

This edition is a scanned facsimile of the original edition published in 1956.

Original language edition, Meister Eckehart Spricht,
published by Verlag "Ars Sacra", 1925

Nihil Obstat: Joannes M. T. Barton, S.T.D., L.S.S.
            Censor Deputatus

Imprimatur: ✠ Georgius L. Craven
            Epus Sebastopolis
            Vic Cap.

Westmonasterii, die la Oct., 1956

CONTENTS

INTRODUCTION

THE present booklet is of a devotional character and is
offered to the public with a view to fulfilling the task which
the pious medieval preacher and spiritual director set himself. Those who wish to study Meister Eckehart's writings
are referred to the historical research on Eckehart's 'system'
which is being presented by the same publisher and gives
information about manuscripts and literary sources.

Born about 1260 into the noble family of Hochheim of
Gotha, Eckehart, at the age of eighteen, joined the Dominican order in Erfurt as a novice. This was one of the most
distinguished orders of the day with regard to knowledge
and the art of preaching.

The Europe of Eckehart's days was the scene of an un-
paralleled struggle for power between the Church and the
political states. From the tragic end of the Imperial house
of Hohenstaufen all through the years of the Interregnum,
the terrible period of strife for Imperial power, the Papal
exile in Avignon, down to the death of the excommunicated
Emperor Louis of Bavaria, the atmosphere was filled with
the terror of war, Black Death, bans and interdicts and all
the horrors of the 'apocalyptic horsemen'.

Yet the same age saw theology reach its peak—High
Scholasticism—and piety rise to a climax of sheer splendour; German Mysticism was born. But this same piety
also produced occasional discords and sometimes even
deteriorated into eccentric revelry and mere sensuality.

But on the whole the spiritual culture of this period
presents a curious counterpart to the outside world with its
problems of hierarchy and state. In the seclusion of monas-

teries, convents and houses of Beguines thousands of pious men and women found an entirely different world, islands of rescue as it were and peace through religion. It is only to be regretted that the withdrawal from the world of these men and women meant that the mass of the people were left a prey to misery.

The cloistered men and women experienced the repose and security which are the gifts of God's Grace, the ever fresh impulse to attune their lives to the key of Divinity, an unending joy in meditation, prayer and writing poetry: in short, a blessed way of life. This quietistic inclination (taken in its widest sense of the word) lacked, however, the reforming element and the drive for great social actions.

Meister Eckehart is the typical child of his time—indeed, in the realm of monks and nuns he is a true king.

We know nothing whatsoever of his childhood, education or his choice of profession. His first appearance on the scene is of one who has come from nowhere. We can judge his personality far better from his writings than from the accounts of his contemporaries. The secret of his 'mythical figure', as Gorres calls him, becomes all the deeper when we consider the tremendous impression which he made. We can say almost with certainty that the man who had such mighty influence on the minds of his time, must needs have been great.

The usual course of education in a monastic order, after the completion of the novitiate, consisted in a study of Theology and Philosophy; the gifted pupils were allowed to follow the so-called general course of study which, for Germans, was taught in Cologne. Albert the Great, the most famous teacher of this town had died as recently as 1280, only a few years before Eckehart, by now probably thirty years of age, put the final touches to his education at the university of Cologne.

We have reason to believe that, between the years of 1290 and 1298 he was Prior in Erfurt and then Vicar in Thuringia; during this time he wrote the treatise which, under the name of 'Discourse on Differentiation' already shows his genius to have flowered into full bloom.

At the turn of the century we find him, 'Frater Aychardus Theutonicus' in Paris, teaching at the most famous medieval school which had, only a generation before, reached its highest peak in St Thomas Aquinas. It was here that Eckehart received the title of Licenciate and Master. We know from the evidence of later sermons that during his stay in Paris he also occasionally took part in philosophical discussions with the Franciscans and defended St Thomas' ideas, which was his duty, seeing that they both belonged to the same order.

Meanwhile Thuringia had been divided into the provinces of Saxony and Alemannia and Eckehart, being a son of the newly created province of Saxony was called home and shortly afterwards, in the year 1303, the Chapter of Erfurt made him their Father Provincial. Honourable though this high office was, it still meant the interruption of his scholarly career. However, those in authority were of the opinion that the Meister's gift of handling human problems justified the change.

The confidence and respect which Eckehart earned in his new position found its expression in the appointment which the General Chapter conferred on him in 1307. He was to add to his sphere of action the deputyship of the neighbouring province of Bohemia. When, however, in 1310, also the Upper German province claimed him as their Superior, the General Chapter refused to confirm this appointment on the grounds that he had been chosen to return to Paris as a teacher.

We can assume that this is the period during which the

Meister began to record his scholarly lectures which, in due course became known as the great 'Tri-partite Works'; in addition to the writings about the 'system' and the commentaries on Holy Scripture, Eckehart, towards the end of his life, also added rough drafts for sermons to be used by his pupils.

This second sojourn in Paris cannot have been a very long one, for after only three years we find that the Meister is back in Strasbourg in the capacity of Prior and Preacher. Arrived at the summit of his career, preaching becomes Eckehart's real vocation and here he achieves his greatest fame.

We will have to recapture memories of churches and chapels of the various orders if we want to visualize the place in, and the audience to which Eckehart preached. There were no less than seven nunneries of the Dominican order in Strasbourg which were mostly filled with the unwedded daughters from the upper classes. It was the 'privilege' of the learned monks of the same order to look after the spiritual welfare of their sisters in Christ.

It is therefore in purely monastic surroundings that the Meister delivered his devotional sermons. As the present day visitor to those churches can ascertain, the interior of these buildings left very little space for the lay-people. This fact has often been overlooked and is one of the many reasons why Eckehart's sermons have been misinterpreted.

The edification of a learned monastic circle obviously necessitated a suitable selection of subject matter. By preaching about moral issues one must lead the way towards religious 'illumination and collection'. There is no need to touch subjects like actual vice, the 'world' and the Devil, nor are social duties, worries and dangers of the worldly life within the scope of these monastic sermons. Although Eckehart followed St Augustine closely in ethical matters, his mind was much less concerned with questions of social struggle than that of his teacher. Himself a monk, he spoke to nuns and Beguines. Such varied subjects as marriage, education, knowledge, economics, politics and art, in short everything which we put under the heading of 'culture' resolve, for Eckehart, into one single note of praise of God who invades the soul and endows it with the inner life and its splendours. In this sphere Eckehart is completely at home and elaborates on a variety of pastoral wisdom; the casting of longing glances at rare rewards, the over-anxious pursuit of mystical experiences and consolations, the over-rated estimation of set rules in the form of spiritual exercises are all to him obstacles on the way to holiness. He advocates true unison with God's will, a steady mind in the face of joys and tribulations and the brotherly spirit of fellowship. These are, in his eyes, the signs of and the means to achieve perfection. He aims at encouraging the inner driving force of the 'divine' in human nature, to the utmost exclusion of hopes of reward, loving the 'good for its own sake'; nothing short of this aim is, according to him, the pure love for God.

Also in the dogmatic realm the unusual approach, peculiar to Meister Eckehart and the contemporary Dominican mystics, can be explained by the consideration which he had for the spiritual edification of his audience. Whilst the commentaries of the scholastic school touch more or less on all philosophical and theological subjects, the spiritual conferences of the Dominicans concentrated on questions which affected the inner life of the religious community. It is precisely this fact which shows up the error, brought about by historical ignorance, that mystics and scholastics stood in two camps hostile to each other; the real issue is that not only were they in no opposition to each other, but that there actually existed a 'personal union' between the two schools of thought. Digging into his teaching-past Meister Eckehart chose whatever seemed specially suited for religious stimulus and encouragement and turned the scholastic Latin into the living and edifying language of his sermons. The deepest mysteries of religion and the longing of the God-seeking mind have always had but one aim: God and the hidden being of the soul and its perceived or anticipated unison with God.

At the same time the average high standard of intelligence amongst his listeners allowed for a concentration of thought which the modern preacher only rarely achieves. The lively interest and understanding which the medieval nuns showed for the deep problems of spiritual knowledge can be tested by the exchange of letters between Heinrich Seuse and his spiritual daughter Elisabeth Stagel; and Meister Eckehart's sermons, treatises and books of recollection, taken down by nuns are yet another proof. At times, however, the zeal of his divine inspiration carried the Meister into such vertiginous heights that it must have left his devout audience in a state of utter dejection. His last conference is entitled 'All-important questions and matters'. The urgency of his message overwhelmed him, when he exclaimed: 'I welcome the man who has understood this sermon; but even had nobody been present, I should have had to preach it to this stick'.

Eckehart was a preacher by the Grace of God. All his writings which have been saved for posterity speak of a power of language the like of which makes him outstanding across the centuries. His way of expression is as pure as can be found only with the classical Greek philosophers, his syntax is clear and supple, reminding one of the best French writers, yet the flight of his thoughts is as bold and high as those of our greatest thinkers. He was a born preacher, taking pride in the most accurate expression of an idea; in his eyes the strongest wording is the best, when it comes to contrasting dramatically the religious and the everyday way of thinking. Yet his sense of good taste and manner never leaves him.

The art of delivering a speech is equal in its greatness to the thought expressed. Eckehart is one of the giants of this world, when his genius for simplicity and logic allows him to survey all things from a high spiritual platform. However, it is obvious that he is not 'everything to everybody' in the sense, that he cannot, by discoursing on all sorts of subjects, leave these, great or small, to the mercy of popular judgment. He can only carry all people with him to God, in whom his soul lives and God in him. All wordly joys and sorrows and even the various religious methods, however holy, pale for this mystic in the face of the essential and ineffable Presence. About our Lady, the 'dear saints', the 'means to attain to Grace' and other devotional exercises he knows as much as is necessary to know for a Catholic thinker. But he maintains that it is wrong to suppose that Christians cannot overrate these things; it happens that the exterior forms are misinterpreted, not in religion, but by many devout people who are to be blamed for concentrating on exercises instead of having their hearts set on God, or as St Augustine puts it: 'they mistake the 'usus' for the 'fruitio'. 'What all the external means cannot give you in the course of years, God can grant you in one instant.' Jesus Christ in his humanity also wished to be only the 'way' to the Father; for you, too, there can be one thing only: the Eternal God within you, who is 'all in all'.

Meister Eckehart has done as much as any man who ever lived for the mental grasp and interpretation of the Inexpressible, the Essence and Life of the Divine Being and the inclusion of Divine Nature in the hidden life of God's children. He can never resist the impulse to lift himself up towards the searing light of religion—the Divine Mystery—however much the human mind is blinded by this 'extreme light which is darkness'. The urge towards religious philosophy is for ever strong in him and he is of the kind of 'poets and thinkers'.

The judgment of the mental achievements of the Middle Ages, known as the scholastic philosophy has, during these last few decades, freed itself of the one-sided and negative criticism to which four centuries had subjected it; we have to thank men like Denifle, Ehrle, von Hertling, Baeumker and Grabmann for this elucidation, though it cannot be denied that even to-day the man of average learning still stands under the spell of this inherited prejudice. The students of higher standard speak now in respectful tones of the philosophical achievements and homogeneous philosophy of life in the Middle Ages, even when it is not their creed; they would learn much more were it not for occasional outbursts of uncritical adulation which stand in the way of honest research.

As for Meister Eckehart, it is fascinating to witness the admiration which un-scholastic circles offer to the 'original German philosopher of the Middle Ages'. It is, of course, the homage paid by modern men to the veiled and uncomprehended scholastic philosophy. At all events, Eckehart in his philosophy is a scholastic through and through.

And yet he would be misunderstood if one saw in him primarily the scholastic whose sole ambitions were speculative studies. As one of the guild of teachers he is only one amongst many and St Thomas Aquinas is far above him when it comes to cool lucidity of thought. But Eckehart is aware of this; he is St Thomas' pupil and a loyal follower as far as his spiritual affinity with St Augustine and the neo-platonic school will permit. Even during his sermons when,

in order to increase his hold on the audience, he pretends
to say something new and unheard of, he knows full well
that close inspection by his colleagues will only reveal a
new and unexpected expression of an old truth. He himself
has often mentioned this curious fact. Modern admirers of
his alleged 'originality' have understood him as little as his
opponents who tried to trip him up. In reality there is
literally nothing in his philosophy or theology which he
could call his own; everything is rooted in the tradition of
the old teachers. In this respect he is the true scholastic;
texts and metaphors from Holy Scripture, the Church
Fathers and School-men as well as the generally acclaimed
sages of Greece, Rome, Arabia and Judea fill at least one
half of his learned writings. Also in his sermons he quotes
very often. His supreme quality, however, which raises him
high above the average is not the result of scholastic
learning nor of studying literary sources, but springs from
the divine gift of his disposition, the experience of life and
his ability to understand and direct human souls. He said:
'one past-master in life is more important than one thousand
school-masters', meaning the scholastic professors! His
thoughts spread their most grandiose wings whenever he is
called upon to speak as a master of life and spiritual adviser,
whether to the inhibited, or half-liberated or to the almost
perfect children of God, his 'dear children', his brothers
and sisters. No scholarly discussions for him, but the appeal
of human being to human being and so we are treated to a
true example of German sentiment.

That is the reason why—though many of his scholarly
writings have vanished—the Meister lives on in his sermons and spiritual conferences even after his tragic end.
Therefore he had no 'pupils' but 'disciples', men and
women who for generations called him their 'great, saintly,
divine master'. They knew why they were so grateful to

him: he had taught them the joys of being Christians by showing them the way to their inner being. They, who had been forced to pay homage to the letter were released to enjoy the unlimited freedom of the spirit of 'divine life'.

They realized that his moral character entitled him to be their leader. He was the living example of the man who is a king, because he has given himself to God and has freed himself of all worldliness. His message was such, that they were certain that God himself had revealed his Mystery to him. Many a legend speaks of this conviction, of which the following is an example:

'Meister Eckehart received one day the visit of a beautiful naked boy. He asked the youth whence he came and he replied: "I come from God". "Where did you leave him ?" Eckehart asked. "In virtuous hearts". "Where are you going ?" "To God". "Where will you find him ?" "In my renouncement of all creaturely ties". "Who are you ?" "A King". "Where is your Kingdom ?" "In my heart". Eckehart said: "Be careful that you share it with nothing and nobody". "I take great care", the boy replied. There-upon Eckehart took the boy to his cell and said: "Take which ever coat you want". The boy answered: "Then I should lose my kingship"—and disappeared. God himself had appeared to Eckehart and had made merry with him.'

Even in his Latin writings, decisive as they are for the understanding of his religious-philosophical system, we encounter not only the 'professor', but also, though naturally more restrained, the human being, great and lovable man that he was. The knowledge of human nature, love and honesty are his most prominent qualities. During his travels, in universities, churches and chapter-halls he had ample opportunity not only to see people but also to know them. Most of his knowledge, however, he acquired by experience. The spiritual problems of the 'devout by profession' held, amongst all others the greatest fascination for him and in this he was an 'expert'. He had a sharp sense of observation and often speaks in a popular fashion, apparently joking yet insisting on his deep morality, but never with bitterness.

It seems that even then the quotation was familiar that 'in the market-place the shilling is of more value than God', and Meister Eckehart even spoke about people 'who, though they are to be commended for keeping away from obviously humiliating vices such as the so-called carnal desires, take little notice of much graver sins, those against the Holy Ghost.' His honesty compelled him to point a warning finger at the clergy: 'There are not many true priests in these lands; I could count them on the fingers of one hand. Who, then is a real priest? It is the man who chooses to remain a priest for the love of God whether he suffers shame and disgrace in his vocation or whether it brings him honour. I am very much afraid that there are few and I don't know whether I am one'.

The deep wisdom of his maxims is exceedingly effective. We only quote a few of them. 'You cannot miss anything while you work with God, nor can God miss anything.' 'The man whose heart is full of love has always something to offer.' 'At times it is more difficult to suppress one word than to refrain altogether from speaking.' 'One thousand Pater Nosters uttered from an envious heart are in proportion to Hell as two to two.' 'Nothing is as sweet and as smooth as the way to corruption and nothing so bitter as to be corrupt.' 'To have sinned is not a sin as long as we are sorry.' A thorough knowledge of human nature easily makes pessimists of us. The deep piety of Meister Eckehart protected him from this danger. Although he realized that 'a struggle exists between flesh and spirit' and that even the prayers of many a devout person reflect more a subtle

selfishness than praise of God, he was nevertheless funda-
mentally an optimist. He often stressed that 'God has made
all things perfectly'. From his studies he was acquainted
with the teachings of a number of antique writers that there
is more evil than good in the world; but Meister Eckehart
had absorbed St Augustine's view that evil is just nothing
and sin, which constitutes evil for the individual is ultimately made by God to fit into the beauty and perfection
of the universe. 'Sin is the greatest of evils', Eckehart said,
but he also said that 'as there is no error without a grain of
truth so there is nothing which is totally evil'. 'No created
being is so base that it could love an evil thing. Whatever we
love must either be good or at least seem good.'

The benevolent smile and humorous toleration with
which Eckehart watched the ways of the world are the
result of this disposition. Yet he does not hold back with
his high moral demands; in fact few men have had such a
pure grasp of the good for its own sake and few have
stressed with more insistence that moral actions must be
directed by God's will. In his eagerness to illustrate how
the reason should have control over the natural desires and
that man should not 'outrun, but follow' God, he tells the
droll story of the woman who bade her boy lead her goat,
called Joan, out to pasture; the animal, however, caught
sight of the leaves on a bramble bush and dragged the boy
across the thorny brush until he cried out: 'Joan, Joan, my
mother said I should lead you, and here you are leading me!'

Occasionally the friendly jest turns into irony, particu-
larly when, as it often happened, the Meister had to deal
with the moral infirmities of devout people; he maintained
that also amongst them it can be noticed that they regard
and love God in the same way as the peasant regards and
loves his milk-cow: 'you love it for the milk and the cheese
which you obtain from it for your own selfish aims.'

He is apt to throw cold water on the contagious spreading of 'mysticism' amongst nuns who, in their eagerness for visions of their Heavenly Bridegroom are inclined to believe in an imagined assurance that they are 'God's favourites, or that God has chosen them to do some special work'. Eckehart is very firm in his judgment of those undiscerning people who, shallow-minded as they are, think that a devout air, special attire or outward works infer holiness. 'One ass knows always how to respect another ass'.

These few examples show how original Eckehart's way of expression was; he himself called it 'rhetorical emphasis'. It is, in fact the weakness or the strength as the case may be, of the born preacher not to shrink from bold definitions and strong language which, if every word were weighed would necessarily appear to be exaggerated. It matters little as long as they fit in with the context of the sermon and serve the purpose of the preacher in church, who has a very different task to fulfil than that of the teacher of science. The famous preachers have always, whether deliberately or by nature, strong colourful language; they must have at their command the gentle whisper as well as the rousing storm of the spirit in order to surprise and frighten and shake the ordinary man into awareness. Not even the greatest amongst the preachers has been spared mis-interpretation, certainly not those of Holy Scripture.

This is not the place to revert to those discussions about Eckehart's general system of thought, the sources or the erroneous and misunderstood parts of his writings, which have been classified in the enlarged and comprehensive edition of this work. The points in question are chiefly statements about the hankering after spiritual rewards, the futility of outward actions without proper disposition, the equality of man with God's Will, and the unity of man in a state of Grace with God and Christ respectively. We only mention what emerges from the study of the Meister's hand-written and printed works: not in one single article of theological doctrine, be it God and his Being, Holy Trinity, Creation, the Incarnate Son, primeval man, sin, redemption, Church, or be it freedom, Grace, virtue, prayer, merit or glory, has Eckehart departed or chosen to depart from the Church's teachings. Even if the Meister had not solemnly affirmed this in the decisive hour of his life, we could, in the light of his writings, arrive at no other conclusion. Eckehart's close friends and the members of his order were of the same opinion.

Fighting on two fronts—against the trend of a coarsening externalism in Christian life and against pseudo-mystical tendencies of his time—Eckehart never ceased to express his fundamental ideas of religion; his power of conviction and the nobility of his character raise him far above the average professional proclaimers of truth. He refused to close his eyes to heretical and moral dangers amongst the apparently allied mystical Beghards and though he ran the risk of being misunderstood he put his trust always with incomparable idealism in the power of truth. Given the opportunity he does not hesitate to draw a sharp line of distinction between Truth and 'those people who are guided by a false spirit, who do not recognize sin when they encounter it, who do not practise virtue but refuse to accept Jesus Christ's sovereignty and who persist in speaking of close intimacy with God, when in reality they are not at all acquainted with him'. Nothing could possibly be plainer than this statement. On the other hand it speaks for his charitable character that such passages occur very rarely in his writings. He is not out to defend the religion of the inner man by polemics nor is he a fighter; all he wants to do is to proclaim his faith. He believes that truth speaks for itself; it needs only to be expressed in words and men will listen to it, but there is no help for those who refuse to listen.

His technique of fighting dangerous tendencies of the period, which were not merely accidental errors, was to make their religious tenor his own and thus show up the heresy. He was accused of being obscure in his sermons, but the deepest motives cannot be put into words: 'If only you could see my heart,' he said, 'you would soon understand me for it speaks the truth and I am willing to pledge my soul that this is so. Truth is noble and if God chose to turn his back on truth I would still cling to it and leave God. But, then, God is Truth.'

Only one who knew himself to be united with the Divine Word and the holiest and sublimest masters could speak thus. That is also the reason why he uses their sayings so easily and freely.

Some students thought they could detect a connection between Eckehart and the 'Schwestrones' who were condemned in 1317 by the Bishop of Strasbourg, Johann von Duerbheim. Not only did Eckehart himself condemn them but the best refutation of this theory lies in the fact that at the time he was called away by his order from Strasbourg to take up a higher position of trust.

We come now to the last phase of Eckehart's life. He had served the Kingdom of God as teacher, writer and preacher. The reputation of the high quality of his exhortations, both in spirit and character has been testified by the convents of Offenburg, Thurn, Innenheim, St Catherine and Oetenbach near Zuerich, where he preached. The nobility of his mind and the purity of his conduct had won for him the respect of the people, to say nothing of the personal love for which a man of his nature must have been very susceptible. The admiration of the nuns was even expressed in poetic language.

> Rejoice in the news
> Said a nun most fair
> Monks to this Recluse
> Are brought through your prayer.
> They have many a good story
> And will speak of Heavenly Glory.
>
> But when they depart
> Keep God in your heart
> Unity with the Lord
> Will be your reward.
>
> Meister Eckehart the Wise
> Will speak to us of the 'Naught'.[1]
> Who cannot grasp this word
> Should make his lament to God
> For the purest Divine Light
> Has not made his soul bright.
>
> But when he departs
> Keep God in your hearts
> Unity with the Lord
> Will be your reward.

When Eckehart, travelling down the Rhine neared his home after many years of absence he had no foreboding of all the heartbreak which was to come his way.

The Meister was in his sixties and his creative power was on the wane. But more than ever was he able to give from the wealth of his wisdom, and his order assigned him the finest field of action: to look after the academic youth.

His essential work was performed, as in the past, in the quiet of the monastic houses. No letters, writings or documents of this period have been handed down to us. But the love which his pupils and his subordinates bore him, even

---

[1] The mystics of the Dionysian sphere of thought called God in his Mystery the 'Naught', because no human word can 'touch his True Essence'.

after his death, speaks far more eloquently than documents. We need only mention blessed Heinrich Seuse who, in his work *Vita* has immortalized Eckehart, by referring to him as the 'great, saintly master'.

Besides his main activities Eckehart continued to preach. It is hardly to be expected that he launched out on new topics and we have proof that he preached some of his sermons more than once; he must have brought his sketches for sermons with him when he left Strasbourg. But whether old or new the ardour for thought of the Divine was for ever young in his soul.

But sooner or later his unlimited idealism was to prove disastrous in this material world. Though the majority of his hearers were equal to the standard of his sermons by having a certain amount of theological knowledge through their professional training, this cannot be assumed of all, inasmuch as lay people had access to the church where he preached. They, too, were attracted by Eckehart's sermons; mystery and obscurity of thought will always draw men and the charm of poetic language may also delight those who can only grasp the approximate idea 'per speciem et in aenigmate'. The Meister had been warned more than once of the danger of acquainting simple minds with the deepest Divine Mystery. He refers to it at the end of his 'Book on Divine Comfort', only to refute it. The traditional story of the visit of the 'eminent cleric' whom Eckehart thanked heartily for his well-meant advice need not be put aside as mere legend. The facts probably are correct and it shows the Meister's polite manners that he thanked the prelate for his good intentions. But Eckehart did not change his views. He said: 'Of great and sublime things one should speak in a great and sublime way, but not keep silent about them. If one were not allowed to teach the ignorant there would be no learned men. If someone has not understood my sermons in the right way it is not my fault, as I have used the right words. St John begins his gospel with the deepest thought that man can express about God—and have not his words, as our Lord's words been misinterpreted ? The loving Clemency of God, who is Truth may grant me and all who hear me that we may perceive our true selves'.

In the year 1323 the General Chapter in Venice heard complaints about sermons in the German provinces which might lead the simple people astray. It is not quite clear whether unwise utterances about the political strife between Pope and Emperor were hinted at or whether the mystical nature of sermons was to be attacked. But it is more likely that the latter was the case because the same year saw the appointment of an eminent Dominican, Father Nicolaus von Strasbourg, a former teacher in Cologne, as Papal enquirer for the German provinces. It seems that the Archbishop of Cologne, Heinrich von Virneburg had launched a formal complaint with the Papal Court. He had marked the beginning of his reign by decrees against the heretical Beghards and had despatched a number of them by having them burned at the stake or thrown into the Rhine. It may well be that some of them, in order to re-habilitate themselves had pointed out a relation between their thoughts and those of Meister Eckehart. The same misfortune befell many an ecclesiastically acclaimed mystic like Heinrich Seuse, Tauler, Luitgard von Wittichen who were suspected of heresy and persecuted during their life-time. The Archbishop was anything but friendly disposed towards the Dominican order and Eckehart, their most distinguished and respected member had been marked out as a target.

The enquirer bade the brothers tell him everything which could add to the exoneration of the suspect. He aimed at avoiding all sensations and at settling the matter within the walls of the monastery. The investigation ended with the declaration of Eckehart's innocence.

This, however, was not in accordance with the Archbishop's aims. Against the Papal investigator he set up an independent investigating commission consisting of two Franciscans who, while the Scotist controversy raged, were Eckehart's avowed enemies. These men soon assembled one hundred statements collected mostly from sermons taken down by nuns and which were to prove Eckehart's heresy. In order to do justice to his order the accused agreed on 26th September, 1326, to submit a detailed defence, in which he expounded the orthodox meaning of the statements. The commission, however, or rather their employer did everything in his power to delay the winding-up of the case and in this way to undermine the Meister's reputation. This endeavour was furthered by two Dominicans, who, though their dubious character has been shown up since by unmistakeable proofs, offered their spying services and for the sake of personal revenge also strove to get the Papal visitor entangled in the unsavoury mesh. He was summoned, together with Eckehart to appear in January 1327 before the Archbishop's court and both protested against the accusations under appeal to the Pope.

Realizing the sensation which this affair was stirring up everywhere Eckehart did not think it wise to leave public opinion in the dark any longer. He resolved therefore to make a public declaration on 13th February in the Church of the Preachers in which he declared that from the very beginning he had abhorred, as going against his cleric position, all deviations from the faith and from high morals; he was ready to refute any errors which judges might find in his writings or his sermons. He was not aware of a deliberate departure from the faith on one single point.

As can clearly be seen, it is not possible to speak of a 'refutation' in the proper sense of the word. Eckehart has never admitted that he had conceived heretical thoughts. As far as we know the members of his order have also upheld this point of view to the last. Yet there can be no doubt that, had Eckehart lived to see the Papal verdict he would have accepted it in submission. There would have been no need to revoke the ever apparent evidence of his clear conscience; not is it the principle of all clerical censorship to doubt that the author acted in good faith—unless he has declared himself explicitly a heretic—but to censure the 'objective' sense of the words, as common sense interprets them or could interpret them.

The official declaration of the attitude of his judges towards the appeal to the Pope had been promised for the 22nd of February. The appeal was to be refused. In this case the administration of justice remained in the hands of the Court of first instance, the confirmation of the verdict was reserved for the Pope.

At this moment of great tension there is a complete blank in the succession of surviving documents. But the following events justify the deduction that Cologne returned a verdict of heresy. The two incriminating witnesses, the Dominicans Hermann von Summo and his accomplice Wilhelm, after the 'great success' of the business in Cologne had made their way to Avignon and the Papal Court either to serve there by 'giving good advice' or to escape the prosecution for certain clerical offences which they had committed within their order. We do not know whether or not they gained influence in the Papal Curia. There was no need for their further incrimination as far more influential circles were at great pains to achieve Eckehart's condemnation.

It availed nothing that the principals of the order took

the part of the hunted man 'in whose faith and holy life nobody could doubt who knew him, be they his opponents or any other person'. The Pope John XXII had the official documents of the Archbishops' Court forwarded to him and ordered an investigation by theologians who were to judge the statements, marked as offensive, as to their heretical character; the Pope himself and his cardinals searched them thoroughly before he gave his verdict, which confirmed that of Cologne. That the excerpts of the Cologne commission were accurate was obviously taken for granted and under normal circumstances this would have been the proper course to take. But unfortunately the circumstances were not normal. Comparing the condemned statements with Eckehart's original works from which they were taken, we find that the Cologne commission has made itself guilty of distortions on decisive points which wrest the entire sense of the words.[1]

On 27th March, 1329, the Pope signed the sentence of condemnation on twenty-eight statements. On 25th April of the same year the Bull was sent to the Archbishop of Cologne with an accompanying letter, bidding him to make public the condemnation in all his parishes. A further extension did not seem necessary under the circumstances and did not take place as far as we know.

Eckehart had died before this decision had been reached. Whether the grief over the sustained wrong had eaten into his heart we do not know but we have every reason to assume it.

This tragic end not only sealed the fate of Eckehart's theological writings which are missing to this day, but indirectly the verdict also affected the person of the Meister

---

[1] I shall endeavour to prove this point in the Appendix of the main work.

and has overshadowed his memory up to the present time. To his pupils, however, and to those who knew him well Eckehart remained the respected master and they spread his spiritual doctrine by quoting and passing on his thoughts, either anonymously or under their own names. They were able to do it because they were convinced that the essence of his teachings had remained untouched in its soundness by the verdict. At the same time it was inevitable that his individuality and unique greatness became somewhat blurred. Heinrich Seuse's vision in which he saw the 'blessed Meister in supreme glory, deified in God' is typical of the spiritual attitude of these circles; Seuse asked the Meister in his vision which he considered to be the 'best exercise' and was given the following reply: 'Let your natural self sink into oblivion, be utterly calm, accept all things from God but not from creatures and with tranquil patience resist all selfish people'.

Those involved in the distressing affair were eager that it should be forgotten as soon as possible. That is perhaps the reason why after only one generation the most outstanding chronicler of his time, the Dominican Heinrich von Hervord could take the risk of ascribing the Papal Bull as having been directed against the Beghards; he suppressed the true facts and dodged the issue in such a way that nobody noticed the ruse. It was many centuries before the Bull could be traced.

In the realm of German mysticism Eckehart's name lived on. The writings of Seuse and Tauler, the 'German Theology' by Frankfurter and the related speculation of the Flemish thinker Ruysbroek are inconceivable without Eckehart's influence. His German sermons were too well known and their propagation could not be prevented. Yet only a handful of men were aware of the existence of his theological works written in Latin. Amongst them was the famous Cardinal and philosopher Nicolaus von Cues who not only found some of them and learned much from them, owing to his unconscious spiritual affinity with the Meister, but he also left to later generations the invaluable gift of Eckehart's extensive works which, in 1444, he ordered to be copied out for his own use. The awakening zeal for research in the course of the nineteenth century resulted in the rescue from oblivion of the pre-Reformation religious past; it was slow and laborious work to collect the writings from libraries and archives. At last the hour of resurrection had struck for 'German mysticism'.

Two men of entirely different character, Franz Pfeiffer and the Dominican H. Denifle must take the main credit for the research made on Eckehart's works, even if some of their inaccuracies had to be modified and adjusted to make way for the restoration of the true picture. This was my endeavour when I published the Meister's 'System' which, in this excerpt, is now presented to a wider circle.

I would not have undertaken this task had it not been for the all too numerous productions in the field of 'mysticism' which have flooded the book-market during the last decades. 'The literature about Meister Eckehart is increasing tremendously and much of it is of inferior quality' —those words are taken from a letter which a distinguished expert wrote to me—and that is putting it very mildly. This 'mysticism' is nothing else but an artificial fabric, offered by our knights of the pen to the public for its amusement and the words are so sweet and even smack of 'religion'! It is utterly irresponsible—and adds insult to injury by referring to H. Denifle—to force the medieval Meister into the rôle of standard-bearer for a 'new' religion, Pantheism, which 'claims' to have 'extracted the original vital core from both the mythical and historical shell of Christianity'. These are the words of one, whose

Eckehart edition runs into two volumes which has been widely read, thanks to the brilliant but sadly biassed translation in which he shows not the slightest inclination to penetrate into the sphere of medieval thought; though he knew the most important writings of Eckehart he ignored them completely, obviously fearing that too eloquent an historical testimony might hamper the propaganda of his creed.

Under these circumstances it is to be welcomed if the plan to publish the complete edition of Eckehart's Latin works is realized. If, however, it is published it will become only too apparent that, as can be seen from Denifle's fragments, one is dealing with a 'scholastic' and this fact might turn the enthusiasm of many an Eckehart-fan into disappointment and alarm, whereas the professional theologians will have ample proof that they were right in contending that, seen through the eyes of theological science, a complete edition of many another scholastic would have been justified; the Meister of Hochheim, after all, is only one of many when it comes to 'scholastic' philosophy and theology.

The medieval thinkers were under the influence of a sublimely spiritual world and lived, as it were, beneath the starry firmament of divine ideas. Every one of them gazed into it in his own way; some were pondering and for ever seeking new and maybe hidden minor sparks of light; others saw in one flash the mighty spirit and this was reserved for the greatest amongst them; they would concentrate in blessed contemplation on single groups of stars which moved them deeply by their tranquil splendour. 'Everyone according to his nature.' The mystics were attracted by the constellation which they called 'Sanctissima Trinitas'; 'the speculation about God's Essence, Holy Trinity, Divine conceptions, the Verbum Divinum, the alliance between God and the world, human knowledge as such and in its relation to God. These were the fundamentals on which they built their teachings: on the pith of the soul, on the birth of our Lord in the souls of just men'. (See Denifle Arch. II, 526.)

'Bruder Eckehart' stands in the front row of these 'mystical scholastics'. What he perceived was not of his own making but the product of past centuries. Yet it was his special message, he was sent to see these things and to speak of them and they made him great.

He emerges as a great man, as the brilliant interpreter of the deep philosophical and theological world of thought. As a young student he became acquainted with them and with a rare power of perception and depth of feeling he absorbed them in order to express them in dignified language as a grown man. Accordingly he is great in his German sermons and writings where, steeped in philosophy he was able to make use of his unique power of preaching and spiritual leadership. Meister Eckehart was also great through his human qualities and as a religious character. Only a truly great man can rise to such ethical heights as are expounded in his works.

I

OF DIVINE BEING

GOD

THE ultimate Reason, the sublime and the essentially Divine in all things are unknown to us. They remain hidden, the eternal Mystery.

God is nameless; his Infinity cannot be expressed or conveyed by words, as everything touching the human soul can be recognized but in finite terms.

About God therefore, we can speak only according to our understanding. There is a wide gulf between his being and our perception. God is 'inexpressible', because all Being in him is infinite.

The Fathers maintained that no human tongue could find words, which reflect the Majesty and Purity of God's Divine Nature and St Augustine exclaimed: 'Whatever we may say about God, no words will ever come within reach of his Dignity.'

'Almighty God is the Pure, Perfect Being, the One Absolute and Indivisible, Infinite and Independent Eternal Self, Truth and Goodness.'—Have we now said something worthy of God ?—St Augustine replies: 'If this is what I said, it is not what I tried to convey.'

God is the Being, the Essence of Being and the Fullness of It, the Entire Being: 'I Am Who Am.'

Creatures *have* life and receive it from God who is Life and the Giver of Life.

Only God is sufficient in himself and unto himself,

whereas all creatures are imperfect and in need of 'something else', their Origin, in order that they may participate, exist and act.

Being and Working is the Self-Same with God and is not subject to change. For him there is neither past nor future, he stands above time, One Single, Eternal Present God, resting in infinity.

Everything under the sun is subject to age and decline, but with him all is eternally new. Time brings two things in its wake: age and decay. Yet with him there is neither new nor old—or rather, he is always New, he always creates, he always conceives and always generates. He does not grow old, nor does he recede or cease to Be.

HOLY TRINITY

God in his Being is living, essential Reason, resting within and aware of Itself, Oneness and Life.

The Father expresses himself in the Eternal Word in ever fruitful reflection of his Person. This same Nature, uniting both Father and Son, whilst formative in the First Person, remains receptive in the Second Person of the Holy Trinity.

St Augustine gives five metaphors when he makes Our Lord Jesus Christ speak thus: 'I have come as a Word, uttered from the Heart; I have come like a shaft from the sun, like the perfume emanating from the Flower; I have come as the Brook from the Eternal Well'. The Pleasure and Love, which Father and Son have for one another, are the source from which the Holy Ghost springs. The Procreation is followed by Love, which acts, as it were, as a firm bond between Father and Son and Son and Father.

It is the Father's Attribute that he was not created, but Is of himself, whereas the Son's Attribute is that he is not of himself, but emanates from the Father, according to the act of Procreation. The Holy Ghost's Attribute is that he did not come from the Father by Procreation, but sprang from Father and Son alike, not by way of Creation, but by Love.

II

OF GOD AND HIS CREATURES

PROCEEDING FROM GOD

GOD in his overwhelming Love was moved to bring to life all creatures which, conceived in Eternity through Divine Foresight, are meant to have a share in his Goodness.

God and God alone is the Reason behind everything, therefore he, the Essential Being, is well pleased with all creation as such and delights in it. Also everything created by him is simply and totally good. Evil, on the other hand, is not part of the creation but the result of the Fall and has therefore no positive Origin. To look, then, for the origin of negation, is to look for naught, for evil is just nothing.

'God has made everything perfectly and all that the Lord has done, is well done.' For he is initially and sublimely, completely and purely Good. He is the only Source of all that is. He, as the Essential Goodness, cannot produce Evil, yet he can use it in such a way, that it is compelled to serve the beauty and perfection of the Universe, God's sole purpose of Creation and Causation. Nothing can do fundamental harm, as both good and evil are used for the benefit of the Universe; though there is evil in the world, harming one person or another, it can never obtain power over the totality.

Everything comes from him, through him and is in him the 'Logos', the Word, the Eternal Source of Being. God is completely in all things, whilst at the same time he remains outside and independent. He is the Essential Being and, consequently, the Universe receives its life from him alone. Yet he is part of no one and comes from no one; everything came from him and that is how 'God created Heaven and earth'.

The 'now', in which God created the world, comprises all 'times'. The last one thousand years are as present to God as this day. The Creation of six thousand odd years ago, when God made the world, is to him present and ever new. Do not imagine that God created Heaven and Earth and all living creatures by making one thing one day and another thing the next. Moses, for the benefit of the people, had to describe the Creation in these simplified and easily grasped terms.

All created things, contemplated by themselves and apart from God are as nothing. While you compare one creature with another, it appears to be fair and representative of something. As soon as you try to liken it to God, it is reduced to a mere nothing. No one creature has independent being, they all depend on God's Presence within them. Should he, for one single moment turn away from them, they would perish.

That is why many a time I spoke to you these true words: 'If someone were to gather up God and the world, he would hold only as much as if he gathered up God alone'.

God is One and no other is. He is 'all in all' and 'all in all things'. In his Person he unites everything in ever renewing fullness. All creatures, in comparison with God are wretched and a mere nothing. Their true being is rooted in God and therefore God is co-equal with Truth.

God Is in all things. We realise that every creature has 'being' and as God is the True Being, he must be in every creature. Yet he is above all things, intangible and existing within himself, the Firm Ground for every creature's anchor.

God, as the Substance, is within all things and all things live through him; and yet he is without, because he is above everything and therefore outside the universe, neither dependent upon nor part of anything.

Those who, for the sake of their own pleasure raise the unreality of mere creatures against God's Reality are wandering away from him. For all that is defective is a betrayal of the Essential.

But God, in wise measure, attracts his creatures by his goodness and leads men of virtue to the recognition of their Supreme Treasure, which is God. In this way all created beings can point the way to God and as much as our life is in God, it is real.

RETURNING TO GOD

Searching for God and finding him is the essence and life of all created beings. Their lives are nothing but a calling for and an eager striving towards him, from whom they came. But these same creatures forfeit their true nature if they are separated from Love, which is God. Never can the soul be at rest, unless it is moving towards God, its First Source, nor will any creature come to rest anywhere else but in God, its First Cause.

Whether you know it or not, whether you like it or not: human nature's innermost core, though not consciously, is aware of God and goes in search of him. God is Love and so lovable is he, that whether taught by joy or grief, every creature capable of love, must needs love him. No created being is so base that it could love an evil thing. The object of love must either be good in itself or at least seem good. Loving *things*—however good they may be—instead of loving the Goodness, makes sinners of us.

The man of virtue should lift up all things to God who made them. For the sake of mankind are they created and one and all should reflect the glory of God. Only when a man's soul becomes one with God, will he be able to trace back all things to their true Origin. Man united with God has a share in God's conception of creatures and in the same measure as his unison with God increases, man's happiness overflows and fills his fellow creatures.

We must love God in everything we see and love everything we know about him. One in all and all in One, so that God is all in all.

Wherever the mind and heart are in search of God, they are sure to find him; should love and thought pursue other, less worthy objects, they too will be found, but they will not lead to God.

Who seeks God and loves him and considers him is with God and in God, who in his turn dwells within his creature.

III

GOD AND THE SOUL

It is far more our soul than our body which makes human beings of us. God has created nothing in his Likeness except the soul. When he made all living beings he found them wanting and so narrow that he would not dwell within them; but then he created the soul in his Own Image so that he could give himself and dwell therein.

When someone enquires after the size of the soul he should be told that Heaven and Earth cannot fill it, only God himself 'Who cannot be confined by all the Heavens of Heaven'. Also the soul is nobler than all material things taken together.

The soul's character is so sensitive that it can soar above the limitations of space. You will notice that when a man's dear friend is thousands of miles away, this man's soul will be carried thither on the mighty current of love. We have St Augustine's words to prove this: 'The soul would rather be where it loves than where it merely gives life'. (It dwells where it loves and identifies itself with the object of its love.)

There is a force in my soul which is forever ready to respond to God. I am as certain as of my being alive that there is nothing nearer to me than God. He is in fact nearer to me than I am to myself. The more a person acknowledges that God is near, the greater is his bliss; whereas his happiness will vanish in the same measure as his consciousness of God's Presence diminishes.

Only God can touch the bottom of the soul; no created thing can penetrate thus far but must remain in the outer realm of matter. St Augustine said: 'Do not go out into the world, but rather enter into your own depths whence you will find Truth'.

IV

SIN AND JUSTIFICATION

GOD is the Beginning and ultimate Aim. Everything which can be brought into relation with this Aim or moves in its direction must necessarily be good. I repeat: 'Everything is good which points to God as its ultimate Aim'.

Because the soul, by nature, is Divine, that is from God—the Heaven of the soul—and the body is earth-bound they are in constant conflict. The body is, in truth, the soul's prison.

Yet it would be a mistake to believe that every evil trend springs only from our nature; actually it is often the result of bad and sinful habits. To be conquered by the Enemy is by no means inevitable as so many people imagine; the adverse powers inflame the evil in us but they are not its cause. A hidden fire glows in the human breast which the Devil likes to stir into a lively flame, but we have the means to resist. God gave man freedom of will, not predestined in one direction or another.

Inclination towards sin does not constitute sin, but the will to commit it, that is indeed sin; also the inner pleasure at bad thoughts is sinful and leaves spiritual death in its wake.

What, then, is the essence of sin? Turning one's back on virtue and eternal bliss is the first deliberate step towards sin. This action is equal to a betrayal inasmuch as man turns away from the 'One', which is God, towards the 'multitude' and thus loses its singleness of purpose. 'Their heart is divided, now they shall perish.'

Every sin has two aspects. The one leans towards inconsistant values such as the world, the flesh and the Devil can offer and the other, in consequence, turns away from the one immutable Goodness. The second aspect gives the reason for and the actual definition of sin.

The study of the soul reveals that sin is the product of pride and trespasses against God's laws. Just as humility is the essential foundation of all grace, so is pride the exact opposite to grace and therefore the root and, as it were, the general background of vice.

St Augustine declares that mortal sin is a malady of nature, the death of the soul, an uneasiness of the heart, a sickness of all energies, a delusion of the senses, distress of the mind, the death of grace, virtue and charity and an erring of the spirit; it makes common cause with the Devil is equivalent to the exclusion from Christian life and, in short, is Hell's prison.

God has created the soul not as just one other part of nature, but he has singled it out for Divine and noble purposes. Were this not so and the soul another unstable created being, it would be too mean and low for God's Condescension.

Those men alone can claim to be noble men who through the Holy Ghost have been born anew, have been changed into just men and have gained new life in God through real contrition. There are three steps by which we are asked to cleanse ourselves from the stains of sin. Firstly by a contrite heart: 'A bundle of myrrh is my Beloved'. You should be sorry for *all* your sins. Secondly by the spoken word through confession: 'Confess therefore your sins one to another and pray one for another that you may be saved'. Lastly by your works of reparation: 'You shall labour and toil like a woman in travail'.

Believe me, the man who is now a sinner can be converted into a good man before nightfall. He may be born into the new life while sitting at his table, eating and drinking.

Human nature is a wondrous thing and its various paths to God are just as wondrous. Some are drawn to God by way of joy, others he draws by inflicting pain and hard blows. At times God works through another creature, at other times without this medium, sometimes also through the word of the preacher; but he can enter into the human heart directly and without mediator. Yet the soul cannot be forced to co-operate, nor will God himself apply force. He gave the soul freedom of choice and he will never wish to influence it against its free will.

Should God decide to create a thousand heavens and earths he would do it by his own Omnipotence and would not need his creatures' help. But should he wish to convert one sinner, he must have this creature's consent, as he will not convert any man without his co-operation.

Sanctifying Grace cannot be merited, for pure Grace is not the outcome of some natural desert in the past but is entirely above nature's potentialities and cannot be gained by righteous deeds. Grace is one of God's gifts and is bestowed according to his Mercy.

Man should not be uneasy about who has been chosen by God and who has not; he ought to offer these matters up to the Glory of God and subject them to his Omnipotence in order that they may be pleasing to him, as they please God. Then he will say with Jesus Christ: 'Father, Thy Will be done in all things, and not my Will'.

Such is God's Nature that he does not go in search of something outside himself but rests within himself. It is his Goodness which makes him communicate with his creatures and seek them out; it is peculiar to his Goodness that It must surge forth wherever It may be. In this way our whole life and being consists in God giving himself wholly to us and making himself known to us.

The receiving of blessings calls for thanksgiving. What could be better than that our hearts, our tongues, our deeds and our writings should resound with the words: 'Thank God'! St Augustine exclaimed: 'No fewer words than those can be found, no happier cry be heard, no greater thing be thought, no better balm be applied'. Why ? Because thanksgiving is nothing else but, as it were, a well-wishing for and a pleasure in all Goodness. And that, surely, is something very natural and lovely indeed, the flower or the fruit of good works, so to speak.

And yet, I do not thank God that he loves me, for perforce he must love and cannot do otherwise; it is part of his being and that is why he gives his Love not as a result of thoughts about himself but rather like the sunshine, which shines upon all things and beings. Rather I should thank him that he is so good, that he cannot help but love and that his Goodness compels him to love me; and I shall pray that he may make me worthy to receive his love and will praise him, who by his very Nature must needs be our Benefactor.

There are four main reasons why we should serve God: The first one is the moral beauty of such a service: 'Beauty without flaw is the work of his hands'. The second one is the satisfaction which this service brings to the server: 'Blessedness is in thy right hand'. The third one is the benefit derived from it: 'Godliness benefits all men'. These three rules can be said to reveal the principle of goodness. But unless the service of God were also made easy, it would be generally neglected and therefore the fourth rule makes the effort light for God's servants: 'My yoke is sweet and my burden light'.

'Good things are learned the hard way,' Seneca wrote, 'But evil is easily acquired and needs no instructor.' Indeed nothing is as sweet and as smooth as the way of corruption and nothing so bitter as to be corrupt. Also nothing is so painful as becoming good and nothing so gladsome as to be good.

Man, for two reasons, fears the Lord: firstly because he is Omniscient, so that no offence can be hidden from him, nor any transgression, not even an omission. 'All lies bare and open before his eyes.' Also because he is All Just and nothing will go unpunished. 'Do not fear those who destroy the body, but rather fear him who can thrust body and soul into Hell.' The rightful dread, therefore is the fear of losing God.

It is of great importance that we should feel sorry for our sins. Contrition can be natural and purely temporal, but again it can be Divine or supernatural. The temporal repentance makes man sink ever deeper and deeper into suffering until he feels so wretched as to despair. The pain drags contrition down so that it cannot rise and thus can bear no fruit. Supernatural contrition, on the other hand, is vastly different. As soon as man is distressed by his sins he rises up, approaches God and eagerly, with a firm will turns away from sin. He puts his trust in God and gains great confidence which in its turn brings a spiritual joy, lifting up and anchoring the soul to God, thereby leaving behind all sufferings and misery.

To have sinned is not a sin as long as we are sorry. But whether mortal or venial sin, if it is done deliberately, it will have to be accounted for in time and in eternity. Who, however, knows how to interpret God's ways should always keep in mind that God in his Love has lifted man from sinful to supernatural life and has raised his enemy to be his friend—an achievement more momentous than if he had created a new world.

When man at last rises above his sins and for ever turns his back on them he has, in the eyes of God, never sinned nor will God for one moment make man suffer f.r his past offences. God longs for a closer relationship with man than he ever had with any of his other creatures. The moment he finds man willing to atone, God will not set against him what has gone before.

Go therefore to Jesus Christ who has made perfect amend for our offences! By him you may make the true sacrifice to the Heavenly Father for all your sins.

Man, with all his sins and shortcomings should lay his

soul into the Wounds of Our Lord Jesus Christ and should commend himself and his iniquity to the noble Mother of God, offering himself up to the Heavenly Father and his Son. In this way we shall partake of Our Father's Love for his Son.

The true lover loves and sees God in everything. He accepts everything as ordained by God, whose will is as a sweet odour to the lover. God's will is all-embracing and is in every single thing, here and there and everywhere, whether small or large, evil or good, adverse or fortunate, bitter or sweet. 'He has poured his will over all his works.'

Whether or not our confidence in God is true and perfect can be easily tested by discovering how much hope and trust we have in him. There is no better way of judging great love than by examining whether one has great confidence.

All those who have risen to unlimited trust in God have remained in his service. He worked great things through them and well knew that their trust was the result of their love.

The loving soul should be completely free and leave all anxieties in the care of God. Forsooth, the God-loving man would show great mistrust if he feared to perish and did not trust in God, who in his generous Mercy and Magnanimity is eager to give far more than we are prepared to accept.

He does not abandon his children whom he made in his likeness. If he does not turn away from the flowers and irrational creatures, but feeds them with dew and clothes them in colours; if he does not forsake the fish in the sea, the animals in the forest and the birds in the air—how much less will he abandon his children, with whom he wishes to share Eternal Joy ?

V

JESUS CHRIST, SON OF GOD

St. Paul wrote: 'Through the mercy of God, I am what I am'.

It is by means of Grace that God, with his wealth of blessings lives in the soul's innermost pith, in the very centre of its spiritual powers and bestows a Divine substance on the soul, ennobling it and qualifying it for a more abundant supernatural life.

Grace turns the man who receives it, into a son of God, a brother of Christ, a Christian.

A soul blessed with Grace is filled with Divine longing, is drawn out of its ambit and lifted through Grace into Grace, which is God. Our Father created the soul for one purpose only: to be united with him. That is the one reason why the Son of God, the Word, took upon himself human nature, so that he might teach us that we can become God's children.

God's Nature, his Divinity must needs work in our souls. He longs so much for our love that he attracts us by every means available, be it joy or sorrow. The effect of his work is that the soul becomes like himself. Divine Nature floods the brightness of the soul and absorbs it.

Our Lord says to every loving soul: 'See, I became man; but if you refuse to join me in my Divinity, you do me a great wrong. For with my Divine Nature did I take up abode in your human nature, so much so that no one perceived my Divine Power and I walked as other men. In the same way you should hide your human nature in my Divine Nature so that no one should see the human maladies

in you and your life becomes Divine—thus all people
recognize only God in you'.

The Father loves only the Son and everything he sees in
the Son. Also the Father is well pleased with his Son and
only with the Son. Therefore the soul should use all its
power to give and sacrifice itself to the Father through the
Son and in this way be loved by the Father when he loves
the Son. That is the reason why we close our prayers with
the words: 'Through Jesus Christ, Our Lord;' thus we
may trust to be heard, for the Father is wont to hear his
Child.

VI

OF FAITH

FAITH carries the soul into those orbits where its natural
powers cannot penetrate. If I am to approach God, the
Essential Centre, likewise distant from and near to all
created things, my natural reason must be lifted up and
drawn by a light shining from above.

Those things which are beyond our natural senses are a
matter of belief and the good man is convinced of the
power of his faith. The less you perceive with your senses
and the firmer you believe the more valuable your faith
will become and the more praise and respect you will
command. 'We walk by faith'; and again: 'Let us draw
near with a true heart in fulness of faith.'

The man who loves God denies himself and rejects the
world. Therefore it is most appropriate that every human
being should be confronted with the Mystery of the Holy

Eucharist, incomprehensible as it is, so that he may learn the art of self-denial and may believe and give himself entirely, body and soul, to God and only to God. For it is love which 'believes beyond doubt'.

The reason why so often we do not find God is because our thought becomes involved in metaphors while we are searching for him, who is Incomparable.

VII

OF INTERIOR SOLITUDE

BEFORE God can enter your soul your creaturely ties must be cast out. Where creature ends, there God begins to work.

God asks no more of you than that you, of your own accord, should free yourself of everything creaturely and leave him to work in you as he wills. The smallest, self-loving reflection clinging to your soul looms as large as God and obstructs your view of God's Fulness. God must yield to such an intrusion, but as soon as it goes, he enters.

Self-love is the root and cause of all evil, depriving us of all goodness and perfection. Therefore, if the soul is to know God it must forget and lose itself; so long as it mirrors its own image it does not see or know God. It is necessary then, that it should lose itself for the love of God and forsake all worldly things so that it may find itself again in God, comprehending him, who in his Truth will reflect the true image of the soul and of all things which it has renounced.

Whosoever disclaims all wordly things in their futility

and accidental existence will find them again in their true and eternal values. Whosoever leaves them in their low and mortal nature will receive them back in God in whom they are true to their real nature.

You will have noticed that at times your heart feels a strange pang and as if withdrawn from the world. That is the effect of Grace, lifting up the soul; for if it is to have a part in God it must be lifted above itself. You can take it as a sure sign that Grace is shining upon you when you, of your own free will, turn away from the transient towards your greatest Treasure—God. Such a seeking soul should keep away from the world so that it can listen to the Holy Ghost who guides the heart towards eternal bliss. The soul opens the door to receive the gift which God bestows on his dearest friends. It wishes to do everything according to the will of its Beloved and strives to keep a clear conscience by repulsing all worldly ambitions and by welcoming all suffering, so that Grace should increase and the evil of carnal desire decline. And in order that the soul should come to realize that it is but a child, living by the Grace of our Heavenly Father, it ought to accept with equal courage everything coming from God, be it love or sorrow.

Man will not find his true self unless he renounces his self-will; only by subjecting it entirely to God's will can it become perfect and real. For man in his perfection is riveted to God's will by wishing to do only what God ordains. Not even the whole array of Our Lady's good works which she had performed in the past could make her worthy to be the Mother of God; but when, as soon as the angel appeared to her, she submitted her will she became in the twinkling of an eye the Mother of the Eternal Word and received God.

Never has God been known to force himself on to an unwilling creature. But wherever he finds a will inclining towards him, there he comes into the soul and dwells therein. Such is the true interior solitude that the Spirit stands immovable like a massive rock and faces the tide of events, be it joy or sorrow, honour or disgrace or even calumny.

So much do the Just hunger and thirst for God's Will and so happy are they in it, that they neither want nor desire anything except what he imposes on them.

Were you to take intense pleasure in God's Will you would be as in Heaven, whatever was done or not done unto you. Those however, who desire something apart from God's Will need only blame themselves; they are for ever in trouble and distress, are more often than not victims of violence and injustice and are always unhappy.

We offend God day and night by our mechanical repetition of the prayer: 'Thy Will be done'—but when it comes to his Will being done we don't like it and are indignant. When our will happens to conform with God's Will we are pleased; but we would like it even better if God's Will were subjected to ours. If you were sick you would not wish to become better against God's Will but you would want him to will that your health be restored. And if you were in trouble you would want it to be God's Will that you should overcome your difficulties. But when God's Will becomes your will then, when you are sick you say: 'It is God's Will', and if your best friend dies you say again: 'It is God's Will'.

The man who by the Grace of God unites his will utterly with God's Will is in need of nothing and will express thus his great longing: 'Lord, show me thy dearest wish and give me the strength to fulfil it.' And as truly as God lives, he will give amply and perfectly in every way.

No human offering is dearer to God than inner solitude. He does not appreciate watching, fasting and praying as he appreciates such solitude, because all he wants is that man should offer him a tranquil heart. All creaturely things must sink back into the darkest shadow so that God the Light may shine: 'And the Light shineth in the darkness'.

If you want to find perfect comfort and joy in God, see to it that you free yourself from all human contacts and their consolations for, believe me, so long as they cheer and please you, the real comfort is not for you. But when nothing can comfort you except God then, in truth he will be your Comforter and with him and in him you shall have joy.

The soul which has received Grace in order that it might, in some measure, know God has grown beyond the limited perceptions of our fellow-creatures with all their frustrations. I make bold to say that such men are completely happy even while still in this world, because every one of their wishes is fulfilled. For they love and see God in everything and therefore at all the times and by the same token they can enjoy all things which come their way.

Such is the perfection to which man can attain: to be separated from and stripped of all creaturely ties, to remain equable under all circumstances; not to be broken-hearted by ill fortune nor to be overjoyed by good luck; not to take more pleasure in one thing than in another nor be excessively happy or in an agony of fear. Whosoever loves truly and sincerely will only see God, the Reality, and beyond it —a sheer void.

Nobody should think that he is incapable of reaching this point: after all it is God who works this wonder. Some people claim that they lack the faith and my answer to them is: 'I am sorry for you'. But should you not long for it I pity you all the more. If you cannot have faith, at least you can long for it and even if you have not the longing you can at least yearn for it!

This is what the prophet means when he writes: 'I yearn, O Lord, for a longing for thy Mercy'.

May God grant us a yearning for him and may he become alive in us!

VIII

THE RIGHT DISPOSITION

THOSE who feel the urge to lead a good life should do what the man does who wants to draw a perfect circle. First he must fix the centre point and only then will he be able to draw a perfect circle. Likewise man must learn in the first place to fix his heart on God, the Centre and thereby on all good works and everything good; because even if he performed great deeds and his heart were unstable, these would avail him little or nothing.

Cling to God and he will give you goodness in full measure; search for God and you will find him and all good things in him. We do not receive our blessings through our works, but by receiving God and devoting ourselves to him. For in the same measure as God is nobler than all his creatures, his works are nobler than ours.

It is essential that we offer a tranquil heart to God; then he will bring his Divine works to bear upon our soul in such abundance that no creature can come within reach of their splendour. God does not consider so much our deeds as our love and devotion and the spirit in which they are done; we should love and see him in all things.

If we distinguish between an inner and outer aspect of a deed, the moral and essential value lies mainly in the inner aspect. Human beings who see only the outward appearance of such deeds will judge them according to human perception: they will seem good or better, bad or worse, whereas God, who sees the heart and the intention, judges in a different manner; he considers the inner value far more and with him it will either be good or evil. Therefore a poor man can also be charitable by only having the will to give. And the willingness and desire of the good man to suffer for God's sake will, in the sight of God be reckoned as real suffering. The patient man's essential quality is patience, whether or not it is put to the test by an affliction. It is not suffering which *makes* man patient, it only reveals the quality to human eyes.

Virtue and morals have their roots in our will and, as St Augustine says: 'It is the will which makes us sin or live a holy life'. You cannot fail if you desire truly and genuinely to have a strong and powerful will. That is within your reach and neither God nor any creature can take it away from you. Man only needs his will to follow God: 'Whoever will follow me. . . .' Through the will we follow God and that alone is sufficient, even if we can achieve no more. To *want* to do something, with a perfect will, to the best of our abilities, and to have done it is, in God's eyes, the same.

Therefore, as long as man wishes to do the right thing he need fear nothing and should not be sad if his works come to nothing. If he is sick and infirm and unfit for outward works, he should concentrate on the interior spiritual work which before God is nobler and greater than exterior deeds. The interior work is made up of the good will and love towards God and it reaps its reward.

The interior act of virtue, in other words the inclination towards the good and the aversion to evil is the Divine element in man and it is the 'Father who rests within', who effects it. As far as man dwells in this love, he really dwells in God and God in him.

Therefore the effect of your love should not be that you enquire into many things and there is no doubt that you should unceasingly do good works; for true love never can be idle. 'Love accomplishes great things while it prevails—and when it declines to go into action it is love no longer,' says St Gregory. God does not tolerate stagnation, futility or sheer emptiness, nor does nature.

God expects every one of our good works to bring glory to him, the blessed expect joy, those in Purgatory hope for help, our neighbours are given a good example and we, who accomplish it hope for reward. Our reward for charity is God. It is not the number, magnitude nor the permanence of the good works on which their merit is based, but on the disposition which 'conceives' the works and which is Love.

Thus all our works spring from the power of love which in its turn is the source of all merits. St Paul says in his letter to the Corinthians (xiii. 2): 'And if I should have prophecy . . . and have no charity, I am nothing'.

So you see there is a work of the interior the meaning of which is to love God and aim at goodness only for the sake of Goodness. The just man is seriously in search of Justice. In the same manner as God does not pursue selfish aims but is pure and free in all his Actions which he accomplishes through Love, so also man, when he is united with God. He too, is genuine and free in all his works and performs them without questioning, through love and for God's glory; he is not in search of selfish aims and God works within him.

Therefore our intentions must be pure and not overshadowed by the expectation of worldly rewards. And that is why a good man will not look for praise though he will wish to be worthy of it; nor will he be sorry that others are angry with him only sad that he deserves their anger.

Man should not seek rewards, understanding or knowledge, not comfort, devotion or peace of mind, but only the will of God. The natural fear, on the other hand, that makes us live in dread of everything that causes harm to our nature, deserves neither reward nor punishment as it is not the product of our free will.

Whilst it is good to serve God in fear, it is better to serve him in love; to combine fear and love is the highest achievement. Yet those on the height of perfection act out of love of the good while those on the lower rungs of the ladder act from fear of punishment. The good man loves God, who is Goodness.

As long as you do your good works for the sake of Heaven or, as it were, approach God and your eternal salvation with ulterior motives, all is not well with you—you are doing tolerably well, but could do much better. And all those who keep free from sin and would only like to be good in order that Our Lord should give them something in return or grant them a favour, are like merchants: they want to exchange goods and, in a sense, trade with Our Lord. They subordinate God to their one aim which is more important and dearer to them than God himself and thus raise the aim to be their deity; as far as they are concerned, they divest God himself of his Godhead. Therefore it is only right that they should not be able to retain their peace of mind, for whosoever loves anything but God is not worthy of him.

Surely our 'works' do not deserve God's gifts and favours. Our Lord wants his friends to do away with this wrong notion and to achieve this, he takes away from them the trust in their works, so that they should trust only in him.

That is the reason why the outward aspect of a deed can never be negligible if the interior aspect is great, nor can the outer aspect be good or great if the inner aspect is mean or non-existent. Therefore man ought to consider not so much what he does as what sort of person he is. If only men and their minds were good, their works would shine brightly.

IX

OF FREEDOM AND SANCTION

THE perfect man has subjected his senses to his spirit, has turned fear into Love and stilled all unrest in his soul. Even if he were free to do evil he would find no pleasure in it and he could not commit sin. Holy Scripture says: 'Walk before me and be perfect'. Therefore, if you want to know whether or not your actions, interior or exterior, are divinely inspired and whether God works within you, ask yourself whether he is the ultimate aim of your thoughts— if so, your actions are good. The soul does not rest until it has broken all barriers which keep it away from God and has reached Divine freedom.

The man is free who depends on nothing and has no obligations. The soul is only free when it has risen above all attachments which are not God and its desires bind it no longer to creatures or to its own self.

In this life we can never hope to free ourselves of all our faults. If we but accepted this truth for God's sake and realized that it is God's will that human nature should be frail (partly through God's Judgment following Adam's fall), we would be resigned to it for the love of God and be justified in putting our mind at ease, finding solace even in misery.

Humility is man's path to God, Mercy the path on which God comes to meet humility.

Real humility makes man conscious of his nature: a something created out of nothing. Consequently he is now as little able to attribute to his own credit the gcod actions which God works in him, as he was before he was created. True humility therefore means total surrender to God and to him alone.

When people say: 'If I have God and his love I can do everything I want to do,' they misunderstand the promise. As long as you desire something which is against God and his law, you lack God's Love though you may deceive the world into believing that you have it. The man who is steeped in God's Will and Love performs with joy what is pleasing to him and refutes all things which are against his Will. Horror of evil and departure from sin are amongst the attributes which go towards the making of the spirit of filial submission; but it is also important that one should overcome one's passions, fighting and uprooting them and being their master.

There are some people who contend that man should attain to such perfection that no attachment of any kind can move him and that neither love nor sorrow should be able to touch him. They are, however, stretching the point too far, for it is my candid opinion that never was a saint so great as not to yield to a stirring of the heart. Do you imagine that you are imperfect as long as words can put you in a happy or in a sad state of mind ? You are entirely wrong. Even Jesus Christ did not possess this power and the best proof is his lament: 'My soul is sad even unto death'. Our Lord Jesus Christ felt so deeply how hurtful cruel words can be that he—Holy Union of Divine and human nature and as such of noblest birth—suffered more grievously than any human being can suffer in utmost pain.

Therefore I repeat my statement that the saint who does not feel pain or joy has yet to be born. Oh, I know our good people would like to attain to such perfection that the things which they can take in with their senses cease to exist for them. They will never succeed. I do not pretend that my senses are so dead to the world that a fearful noise gives me the same pleasure as sweet music, but at the same time I do suggest that we ought to get thus far that our God-made will should free itself from all natural pleasures and keep itself at God's disposal, so that when he in his Foresight thinks it expedient to call halt to our will, we may say: 'I do it gladly'.

Perfect virtue is inseparably bound up with a continuous struggle against our senses. It is very easy to speak about virtue, yet it is very rarely found. If you want to see whether you have perfect virtue, examine yourselves as to whether you are inclined to prefer it above everything, whether you do your good works without great effort and without having in mind a special resolution or a high moral aim. By frequently repeating these acts, one by one, they will become important to you and a wholesome habit. In this way goodness will develop of its own volition through love for virtue and not for the sake of mere why's and wherefore's. Only then will you have perfect virtue. Thus we should always advance and pursue the indicated path, yet there never will be a limit to our progress.

Never must we be satisfied with our success nor ever stand still. This life is not static. Whosoever wants to conquer the Devil and do signs and wonders without guile should take up the daily struggle against sin—the Devil's own weapon—and have patience in adversity.

Some people have more flaws in their character than others. Through our contact with the material world such attributes of character as temper, vainglory or sensuality or whatever they may be, are aroused. These are very often only a shortcoming of our nature inasmuch as man's natural disposition may be tending towards anger or pride or whatever it is and he may try not to yield to this sin. Such a man, compared with one who is not so sorely tempted, deserves far more praise and his reward will be greater, his virtue is much nobler. Therefore it is essential that man should direct his will towards God and focus his mind on God alone. Then he may go peacefully on his way and need not fear nor wonder whether or not he is on the right path. Were a man to decide which road to take and deliberate how he should put one foot before the other—he would never reach his destination. As long as you know the direction and follow it, you will arrive where you want to go and that is the best you can do. By leading a normal Christian life and not attempting to do something spectacular, you will succeed.

The best thing, to my mind, is for man to put himself entirely in God's hands, accept everything, including disgrace, trouble and grief as coming from God, welcome it and bear it with joy and gratitude, letting himself be guided by him instead of trying to direct his own life; then he can also accept honours and fortunes. Should, however, dishonour and misfortune befall him, he will suffer them gladly. I am convinced that nothing can hurt me, except sin.

If something good happens, you can accept it as long as you are willing to accept unwelcome things in the same spirit. And in this way you can enjoy food and drink, friends and relatives, and everything which God either gives or takes away. Those of us who value material things such as particular surroundings, customs, people or worldly achievements, or even worse, those who are content to wallow in discomfort, poverty or utter disgrace can find no peace of mind. They seek to find God by wordly ways and means, and the further they go on that road the less they find peace; they are like the man who has taken the wrong turning and the further he advances the more he loses his bearings. It was St Chrisostomus who exclaimed: 'Truly it is madness to honour the saints and not to love holiness which makes the saints so lovable'. We must first love saintliness and only then the saints, just as we must begin by wanting goodness in general and then we can proceed to love this or that thing for its goodness.

Everything which we can perceive with our senses in this material world has been ordered and set up for only one purpose. It is to lead the outward man towards God and prepare him for a spiritual and good life instead of losing himself in unworthy companionship; this order should, as it were, restrain man from giving himself up to mundane things, so that when God wishes to dwell in him, he may find man ready and his real self not in need of being disentangled from pure materialism. If we are very much attached to worldly matters it will be difficult to turn away from them. The deeper the love the greater the grief when we must part.

Now you can see God's purpose in creating the material world, against which he has set the practice of virtues such as praying, reading, singing, watching, fasting and penitential and other devotional exercises, in order that man should keep away from alien and ungodly influences. But let him not be deceived into thinking that he leads a better life merely because he fasts and does good works; it is only when his disposition towards eternal love grows and his love for passing things diminishes that he can take it as an indication that he is on the right path.

You should keep in mind that God is more pleased with a short prayer coming from a man in harmony with him, than with a long prayer uttered from a restless heart; and in saying this I want to impress on you that one thousand 'Our Father's' coming from an envious heart insult God and bring damnation. The man, however, who is at peace with God is firmly poised in eternal life, where calm and stillness reign.

When man realizes that God's spirit is not active in him and that his inner self's intimate knowledge of God has flagged, it is most important that he should perform devotional exercises specially suited to develop his spiritual strength; they must not, however, be done for their own sake; on the contrary, they should enable him to keep away from material influences and cling so closely to God that his soul is ready to receive God whenever he wishes to return and accomplish his work of salvation.

The discipline of your natural self is necessary because your flesh is always in conflict with your spirit. The body is made of more robust material than the spirit and the relation between the two is nothing short of a permanent fight. The body is bold and strong as it is 'at home' in this life and its origin is the earth; the world with all its kith and kin like food, drink and sensual well-being are its friends. But all these are enemies of the spirit which dwells, as it were, in a foreign land whilst here below; its home and its kinship are in Heaven whence it came. Therefore, in order to help the spirit whilst in exile and to strengthen it against the onslaughts of the body, we must practise penance, thus subjecting the material self into submission and bringing victory to the spirit.

The strongest fetters, however, which will curb the body are the fetters of Love. It is the best way to conquer the body and keep it under control and that is why God uses above all Love in his pursuit of man. Who surrenders to Love carries the heaviest shackles, yet the sweetest burden. It carries us further and brings us nearer to God than all the exercises and mortifications that we can endure. The loving creature can bear and suffer joyfully whatever destiny God has decreed for him. Nothing will make us so inherently God's children as this sweet bondage. Whosoever is treading this path need not search in other directions. Who has been caught in this net will be captivated, body and mind, and will surrender his whole being to God. Look out then for the net and when it closes in on you, rejoice in your captivity which will give you freedom.

May he who is Love help us to gain freedom through captivity. Amen.

X

OF MYSTICAL INTERCOURSE

'By entering the soul, God cultivates the soil, from whence a Divine fountain of love springs; it carries the soul back to God.' These are the words of a holy brother.

In this way God performs a Divine Act; this, however, is not accomplished through our perception, limited as it is to finite terms; but by the Supreme Divine Power—Love. Its rays, reflected in God, shine upon the soul which, through the power of Divine perception is lifted up to God and united with him. And God endows the soul with supernatural strength and Divine life and henceforth it lives according to God's decrees: it has found its first Source where it can be supremely happy in blessed unison with God.

When the soul is gathered up in God's loving embrace it rises up and stands in perfect beauty and bliss. The senses are mute. The knowledge of God becomes immediate and independent of visual impressions. When the soul has reached this pure realization of God, it knows him in his Unity of Nature and Trinity of Persons. His Will and the soul's will are caught up in the same current, embracing in real union, touching and becoming as one: God has given the soul some of his Divine Essence. He considers the creature and infuses it with his Nature, whilst the soul contemplates God and receives from him its true character. God is present where I am, and wherever he is, I am to be found. What is his is also mine and as I love all that is mine and my love is returned; I am being drawn into the loved Object and absorbed by it. Through love we become divine in union with God as far as creatures can achieve this. What God is by Nature, the soul is by Grace.

Yet this communion with and working influence of God can only be experienced by good and sincere men. Who wants to hear God's whisper must have silenced all other voices; the noble life and teachings of our Lord Jesus Christ must above all things become alive in the man.

Those people whose thoughts and ambitions are directed towards the transient world have no knowledge of the interior man; moreover the will is the fertile soil which produces love. Who has more will has also more love. Yet no one can assess how much love his fellow-creature has: it lies hidden in the soul where also God is hidden.

It is, however, vastly different whether the love is kept secret or whether it bursts forth expressed by gentle emotion, great fervour or loud jubilation; these rapturous declarations, forsooth, are by no means proof of great love. It is sometimes the sensual nature of the lover which compels him to show his extreme pleasure in religious devotion. These may be inspired by a Divine impression upon the soul, but again they may come from the senses and those who show much fervour are not always the truest lovers.

Divine Love is given to those who respond to God's call and allow themselves to be severed from their wordly ties. When, however, this love grows stronger and the religious feelings and sentiments diminish, will it become apparent whether or not the soul possesses the real love, when it is entirely loyal to God who has deprived it of these consolations.

After all, every spiritual experience and love, however happy they may make us here below, are only a foretaste of things to come. Complete joy will be ours only in Eternity. It is typical of human beings that their will (or their love)— as in the instance of St John and St Peter—'outruns' their knowledge; in other words: we can love God in a direct way in this life, but we can have no direct knowledge of him whilst we are on this earth. 'That other disciple did outrun Peter and came first to the sepulchre.'

Our revelation of God can never, in this life, be so complete that it is not a mere nothing, compared with his reality.

It is written of Mary Magdalen: 'But Mary stood at the sepulchre without, weeping'—as if the evangelist wanted to intimate that she wept because she was still 'outside'. She, who loved God with such a burning love is the true picture of the loving, God-seeking soul. She always 'stands weeping' whenever she finds herself outside and not within God. She 'stands' though, always as it were in God's Presence, but she 'weeps', because she has not been absorbed in him. As long as man is growing towards God, he cannot see him and as long as we are on our way towards God, we cannot fully have him.

'Do not touch me', said our Lord to Mary Magdalen, for (to your preparedness) I am not yet ascended to my Father.'

May we leave this lower nature behind and have full knowledge of 'Thee, the only True God' and may God help us by his Power. Amen.

XI

OF PRAYER

GENERAL PRAYER

Do you know the signs by which I recognize a good man? It is not by fasting, almsgiving or self-chastisement that he will reveal himself, only by his prayers. The man who uses prayer, this surest of all ways to reach God and to speak to him in close communion, is to my mind the best man.

What we have said of outer works also applies to praying. Keep a pure heart, fixed in God and all will be well with you, even if you perform no outer deeds. On the other hand a prayer, merely spoken, will have no echo in the heart and no cleansing effect.

Only by praying for God's help can we hope to retain the use of our honest free will against the temptations of the Devil. Unless a soul is sustained by Grace, it cannot possibly be without sin. God ordained after Adam's fall that no man should come to him except by Grace and that can only be obtained through prayer, the cleanser of daily sins and bulwark against mortal sin.

We can reach four main stages of Grace through prayer: remission of sins, decrease of temptations, closer contact with spiritual things and eternal salvation. The real prayer is based upon the following conditions: (1) Be charitable and good to your neighbour; 'A prayer is good when it is accompanied by fasting and almsgiving'. (2) Long-suffering and patience in adversity; 'In the sight of God I let my prayer surge up and speak of my sorrow'. (3) Pureness of heart; 'And when you multiply prayer I will not hear, for your hands are full of blood'. (4) Constancy in prayer: 'pray without ceasing'.

We must begin by praying for the remission of sins and this is of special importance to those who have only recently been converted from a sinful life. This is a blessed prayer intermingled with tears of repentance which rises up to God; it is unthinkable that this prayer will not obtain the Grace of God, his forgiveness and eternal life.

The next step is to make a resolution or even a vow to abstain from evil and maybe even to deny oneself something pleasant which one could rightly enjoy without committing sin.

Further up the ladder of perfection we can pray for others and perform thus an act of brotherly love; when we give thanks to God for his Goodness we say the best and noblest prayer amongst those just mentioned.

The next prayer is the 'Our Father', the best of the fixed prayers, given and taught by our Lord himself. It contains everything we need for body and soul.

There is at last the burning prayer, without words, coming from the heart in true devotion; it brings tears to the eyes and represents the most perfect way in which we can pray.

The spoken prayer, appointed for the different seasons and forms of worship has been set up by Holy Christendom so that the soul should collect itself and draw away from the senses and the transitory things of this world. At the same time we should endeavour to find God in all things, be they natural or spiritual.

Even if a man could call all powers his own, he should consider himself a beggar standing outside the gates of Heaven and, holding out his hand, asking for God's Grace as if he were begging for alms; for Grace makes us the children of God.

Those amongst us who are at peace with God will feel at home everywhere and with everybody. But those with a restless mind will feel out of place wherever they go. The inner peace is an integral part of the chosen ones in whom God lives in his Truth and these men will be one with him, whether they be with their fellow-men, in church, in the street, in the desert or in their monks' cell; all their actions will not be so much their own, but rather the outcome of their unison with God.

To be sure, it would never do to have the same respect for all occupations, places and people alike; obviously praying is more beneficial than spinning and the church is a more dignified place than the street. But you should be able to retain the frame of mind in which you were in the church or in your cell and carry it amongst the people into the bustle of the world; above all you should try to maintain the same disposition towards and serious contemplation of God, wherever you are.

Rest assured that if your mind is set in this way, no one will be able to intervene between you and the All-Present God. Yet when he is not in you and you attempt to reach him through the medium of the outside world, its works, people and places, you may well be prevented from finding him. In this case not only bad company, noisy surroundings or angry words will hinder you, but even good company, the quiet of the church or good works will not bring you any nearer to God. For you are a hindrance unto yourself. Had you centred your life in God, you would be perfectly at ease everywhere and with every type of person. Were God in you, no man could take that away from you nor could anyone prevent you from pursuing your aim.

The man into whom God has entered in his Reality is absorbed in God's Divine Nature; all things reflect his Glory and have a Divine flavour. Likewise, nothing except the object of his love will appeal to the man whose heart is alight with a burning love and he will always be conscious of it. In fact wherever and with whom the man may be or whatever he may be doing, his love is with him all the time and in everything he sees the picture of the beloved. The greater the love, the more it is ever present. Only the man who thus sees God's Presence in all things knows the true peace of mind and carries Heaven in his heart.

This perfection, however, is not acquired by fleeing from the world and retiring into the desert. No! one must learn to have an inner solitude wherever one may be.

PETITION

You need not tell God what you need and what you desire. He knows it all beforehand. Jesus Christ said to his disciples: 'And when you are praying speak not much, as the Pharisees. For they think that in their much speaking they may be heard'.

When you ask God to grant you a favour, your mind should be lifted up towards him and not weighed down by worldly cares; though a great longing should fill your heart, yet it should be tranquil in true peace. An essentially true and pure petition is but a longing of the mind for all Heavenly things.

Also it is very important that you should turn your thoughts frequently to Jesus Christ and his humble patience in all his actions and sufferings. We cannot please God if we don't devote our mind to his Son, who is the Gate through which we enter eternal life.

You should only pray for things which add to God's Praise and Glory, which are useful to you and beneficial to your neighbour. Your prayer, however, is really good, when it requests nothing. If I am part of the One to whom all things, whether past, present or future are ever present, they must all be within my reach, as they all have their orgin in God and therefore, as it were, in me. When I solicit help for no one in particular my prayer becomes stronger whereas I touch the very essence of prayer when I desire nothing and ask for nothing.

Our Lord said: 'Whatsoever you shall ask the Father in my Name, that I will do'. St Augustine elaborates on the words, 'in my name', as follows: 'His Name is Christ, King and Saviour of souls. If we therefore ask for something which is not for our real benefit nor for our salvation we do not truly ask in the name of the Saviour'. In other words, every petition which is good for our soul is a prayer in the Name of Jesus and will be granted. If our prayers are not granted it is that we are asking for something which would be detrimental to us.

When we call to God and have him in mind, he will hear us. When, however, we pretend to call for God but actually have worldly ambitions in mind, we do not really call for God at all; instead we think only of the object for which we pray and in this way treat God like our servant.

The best prayer that a man can utter contains only one wish: 'Lord give me only what thou willst me have, and do unto me according to thy Will'. Thus a good son prays who can truthfully call God his Father and who honestly can say: 'Thy Will be done on earth as it is in Heaven'; in other words, God's Will should be done in temporal, human and wordly matters as it is done in Divine, super-natural and eternal things.

We ought to have nothing at heart, nor ask or search for anything but the will of God. Whoever prays in this way will undoubtedly have his wishes granted, simply because he seeks for and rejoices only in the will of God. This is the only test which a pious man acknowledges when he asks not for this or that, but simply seeks to please God and do his will. If, however, he does ask for some special thing, he does it calmly and with diffidence, leaving it ultimately to God's Pleasure whether or not he will give it.

Furthermore we pray: 'Give us this day our daily bread'. We are not told to pray for money or pleasures, but for bread. A disciple of Christ should ask for his daily bread, but beyond that he should not cling to this temporal life; rather, he should pray for a speedy coming of the Kingdom of God and yearn, with the apostle, to 'become as nothing and be with Christ'. We should never pray for transitory things; it does not behove us to approach the Eternal God with such trifling requests. If we pray continuously for temporal things, God's Love for us must diminish because we love him less, or as St Augustine puts it: 'Too little does any man love thee, who loves some other thing together with thee'.

The man who seeks nothing and whose mind is set on God and his Truth grasps and shares all things with God in his Divine Heart; we can say therefore that whoever searches for other things as well as for God, will not find him, but he who searches only for God will find him and, in addition, all things that God has to offer.

XII

CONTEMPLATIVE—ACTIVE LIFE

THE man who wants to love perfectly must set his mind on four spiritual qualities. Firstly a true inner seclusion from all other creatures; secondly his life must resemble Leah's life, which, though active, was touched by the Holy Ghost and prepared to receive him. Thirdly he must lead a truly contemplative life, comparable to Rachel's life and lastly

his spirit should soar to ever higher spheres of love, sup-
ported by God and united with him in eternal bliss.

There are some people who would like to jump to the
conclusion that they are entitled to free themselves from
outward works. But that must not be, for Jesus Christ said:
'So let your light shine before men'. The words were aimed
at those who live a contemplative life and have given up all
attempts to do good works, thinking they are no more in
need of them and have risen above such trifles. And yet, is
not the whole life of Christ and of his Saints a reminder of
the type of life we should live ? He told every one of them
to go out and teach the multitudes. St Paul said to Timothy:
'I charge thee . . . preach the word'. It was only after the
Holy Ghost had descended on the disciples, that they went
out and worked wonders. As for Jesus Christ himself—
from the beginning when he became man and brought
humanity back to God, he worked for our salvation until
the end when he died on the cross.

So also was the whole life of Mary (the Mother of Jesus)
dedicated to warning mankind against all imperfections.
She lived amongst the people in order that they should be
drawn to God by her good example. She comforted the
afflicted, strengthened the people's faith and never refused
her advice.

Nowadays many people, apparently virtuous, flee the
world and hide in monasteries and cells, hoping to be rid
of worldly temptations. If their aim were to seek out God,
well and good, but it is to be feared that they think more of
themselves than of him.

We should judge our works from three different angles:
that they be done in an orderly, honest and reasonable
fashion. By orderly I mean, that you know what your next
act will be while you do the present one; by honest I mean,
that at the time you know of no better work which you could

perform. To act in a reasonable fashion is to become aware, through hard work, of the life-dispensing Truth and its Blessed Presence. Wherever these three conditions are fulfilled, they bring God as near to us and give us as much devout pleasure as Mary Magdalen felt in her chosen solitude. Whereas contemplation serves only your own private purpose, the active practice of virtue will enable you to serve a great multitude. It is not within our limited natural powers to keep free from worldly misery and sorrow; nevertheless every well-disposed soul is longing to fast and watch and to be delivered from carnal desires, so that it may concentrate on God from whom it springs. As the soul is a spirit and sister of the Angels, it would like to live an angelic life. But whilst it is weighed down by the body it must bear its sufferings and fight a daily battle against its enemies. It must force itself into turning its attention to those things which are, after all, a part of our human frailties. We must, perforce, also consider the needs of our body.

You will perform a worthier deed if you feed a hungry man than by practising inner contemplation. Even if you were in ecstacy as it happened to St Paul and you knew of a man who was in need of food, you would do better by showing the hungry man your great love by feeding him, than by remaining in your ecstacy. Do not imagine that you will receive less Grace by acting in this way. Whatever a man abandons for the sake of love, will be given back to him in the fullest measure. Jesus Christ said: 'And everyone that hath left . . . all for my Name's sake shall receive a hundred-fold'.

XIII

IMITATION OF CHRIST

THE Teaching Brothers maintain that God would not have allowed his Son to become Man, had it not been necessary for the redemption of mankind.

Our venerable Brother in Christ tells us the story how, for five thousand and two hundred years our Heavenly Father had done everything in his power to draw mankind into Heaven—and failed. When the Son saw how grieved the Father was, he said to him: 'I shall take Adam's sins and their consequences and twine them into a rope. Thus will I pull humanity into Heaven'. And he descended from Heaven into the womb of our Blessed Lady and took upon himself our human nature. He was exactly like one of us with all our ailings, only he was free of sin and of that folly which is Adam's legacy to us. The Son of God intertwined his words, his deeds and his suffering humanity into one strong rope by which he raised us with his loving wisdom, until at last the bloody sweat poured from his Sacred Body. He had been trying for thirty-three years and still saw no result. Yet he sensed how the people were moved and wished to follow him. Therefore he said: 'And I, if I be lifted up from the earth, will draw all things to myself.' And he was stretched out on the cross where he put aside his Serenity and all things that could hinder him from drawing us. And from the third until the ninth hour when he gave up the Ghost, he drew more men unto him than in the thirty-three years of his life.

As the sun draws the earthly mists towards the sky, so the intensely burning love of our Lord's pierced Heart—like flames leaping from a glowing forge—drew all those men towards him, who wept over his Passion and Death. They will be saved through him unto Eternity.

And thus, dear soul, observe how supremely merciful God has been to you! He gave you freedom of will—which you used in such a way, as to earn for yourself eternal death—and he himself redeemed you, washed you in his Blood and freed you from original sin. He wants to forgive you every time you ask for his Grace. He was without guilt and suffered for yours, as if it had been his own. He atoned for your sins, as if he had committed them and you reap the merits of his Works as if you had performed them.

Our Lord said: 'Who wants to follow me, should deny himself and take up his cross'.

We are to take up Christ's Cross—our cross—by thinking frequently about his Passion, by loathing sin, by renouncing worldly pleasures and by mortifying ourselves, yet loving our neighbour and helping him in every way.

I beg you from the bottom of my heart: consider that we, mere human beings, have no reason to complain about hardships and bitter sufferings, when we remember that our Lord of Divine Substance who will be surrounded by the splendour of his Saints on the Day of Judgment, condescended to take upon himself the mortal form of our low nature. Surely, if we ponder over this Mystery, our troubles will seem much smaller! The devoted knight disregards his own wounds when he sees that his King has been wounded and remembers that this same King has never offered him a drink which he has not tasted first and expected nothing of his servant save what he had done and suffered himself.

It would avail me little if God's word had become Flesh in Jesus Christ and I did not do my share in making him live in me, thereby becoming God's son and heir. Holy Scripture states: 'The Word was made Flesh'—in Christ, the First-Born—and then only goes on to say: 'And dwelt amongst (in) us'. By making the Word dwell in us and accepting thereby the filial relationship to God, we become his children.

By practising faith and doing good works in this life we affirm that Jesus Christ is 'the Way', as far as merits are concerned and he is 'the Truth and Life' in the next world where we receive our reward. One commentator explains that Jesus Christ is 'the Path which does not lead astray for those who seek, the Truth without deceit for those who find him and for those who persevere he is Life without death'. He is the End of the road which we should follow, the Aim which always should be before us and with which we shall be united in its splendour, as far as we are worthy of such a unison.

Therefore we should not become involved with our fellow creatures, but only with Christ, our Father and Succour who is the Way to his Father. As I have told you before, Jesus Christ became Man for one reason only: that we, by his Humanity, should return to God the Father.

We should pray to his Humanity, as being the Temple, which his Divinity chose while he dwelt on earth. Pursue the Man until you find God, whom all disciples of Christ should seek wherever they go. We are not, therefore, to be content with being merely human, for Christ himself indicated the path to God: 'I am the Way and the Truth and the Life. No man cometh to the Father, but by me'. When Christ's disciples loved him, the mortal man, he spoke thus to them: 'It is expedient for you that I go'. For, though he was the noblest created Being, which God could have given us, he was yet by the fact that he was 'physically' present, an obstacle to the disciples. He gave them courage by telling them: 'It is expedient for you that I go; for if I go not the Paraclete will not come to you'. I personally think that he meant that natural love, even if it is love for the man Jesus Christ, hinders us and delays our coming to God. The love for the Human Creature and the Bodily Presence easily can impede the growth of the purer love for his Divine Being.

The Imitation of Christ does not imply that we must speak gently, assume a pious mien or parade great holiness; nor does the realization that our names are known far and wide mean anything or that God's friends are fond of us; it is even of no importance if God himself seems to cherish and spoil us so that we imagine that he has forgotten all other creatures but ourselves and that we need only wish in order that we shall be granted everything this very instant. Oh no! this is not the real thing nor is it what God expects of us; that is something entirely different.

To imitate Christ means to be detached and unshaken in the face of calumnies, of evil inflicted by other men and not even to waver when God actually withdraws his consolations and it seems as if a wall had risen up between him and us and he had abandoned us in the struggle for our needs, as Christ was forsaken by his Father; this is the moment when we should seek refuge in his Divine Nature and say with him: 'Father, thy Will be done unto me'.

Jesus Christ has a great following whenever he leads the way to health and prosperity, to riches and pleasures; but when he leads us towards suffering and adversity: 'This saying is hard and who can hear it?' and so 'they also go away'. Yet, every man who follows in the steps of the Lamb of God can be sure of himself and full of hope! 'If God is for us, who is against us?'

The man whose soul is sown, like a seed of corn, into the soil of Christ's humanity must, like the seed in the parable, die, so that it may bear fruit. In other words: whatever we suffer in the way of cold, hunger, thirst, disdain and undeserved (yet sent by God) adversities, we are to accept willingly and joyfully, as if God had created us so that we may suffer. We are not to seek or desire our own ends in Heaven or on earth. All our sufferings should seem to us as a drop in the ocean, if we compare them with Christ's Passion. Many a man may be discouraged when he thinks of the bitter life which was our Lord's lot. The human being may not feel the strength in himself or the inclination to follow his Lord and many may imagine themselves very far from God and incapable of following him. No one should think thus!

We ought never to imagine that we are far away from God because of our weakness or our ailments or whatever it may be. He stands by the afflicted and comforts them: his Name is 'Comforting Spirit'. 'I shall be with him in his affliction,' he promised. As for the harsh demands which the imitation of Christ involves, mark my words: take note and hold on to the particular way which God encourages you to take. St Paul explains that we are not intended to reach God all in the same way. If you find that your life is not bound up with many outward works, much trouble and privation, you can still be at peace and make the most of small offerings. Unless a man feels a special urge (sent by God), to do great works and has the strength to perform them, he should refrain and not endanger his interior life by forced activities.

Now you will say: 'If these works were not important, why did our ancestors and many Saints perform them?' Remember that our Lord gave them ways and means to achieve much. He wanted them to do all they did, in order that they may be saved. Yet God has not made man's salvation dependent on definite rules.

God has seen to it that all good ways hold the essentially Good; one good thing cannot be in conflict with another good thing and people ought to keep this in mind when they see or hear of a good man who does not conform to their rules. We should respect everybody's customs—which is a true devotion—and not scorn their ways. One man's meat is often another man's poison.

Man must do one thing at a time and not attempt to do everything at the same time. Do one thing, accept it from God, cherish it and do it wholeheartedly. By doing one thing well, you include all other things. Make one way your own, adhere to it and make good with it. Do not begin one thing to-day and another to-morrow and be not uneasy lest you have missed something. You cannot miss anything while you work with God, nor can God miss anything.

Accept one good way from God and draw everything into it. Should, however, one thing not fit in with the rest, you may take it for granted that this thing was not sent by God. Our Lord said: 'Every kingdom divided against itself shall be made desolate,' and he also said: 'He that gathereth not with me, scattereth'. God gives to every man what is best for him, of that you may be sure.

A change in our mode of life usually unsettles our habits and our mind. As long as your present way of life is good and laudable and directed towards God it can give you everything which you may seek in a different setting; not all men can follow the same way.

The same applies to the imitation of the austere way in which some of the Saints lived. You may love their ways and it may be to your liking—but you are not to imitate them!

Now you will say: 'Yet our Lord Jesus Christ had the best way in all things and we are supposed to imitate him'. That is perfectly true; we should follow in his footsteps, but not in all things. Our Lord fasted for forty days and no one should attempt to follow him in this. Christ did many things but he wants us to follow him not so much in the letter, but rather in the spirit. That is why we should try and use our reason in imitating his Way. He is far more concerned with our love than with our works.

Jesus Christ fasted for forty days. Follow him by making up your mind which way is best suited to you and then keeping to that, watching yourself closely. It is more seemly that you should keep a detached mind than that you abstain from all food. At times it is far more difficult to suppress one word than to refrain altogether from speaking. A man can bear more easily a self-imposed chastisement than the smallest insult; also it is far more difficult to be alone in a crowd than to be in the desert. Oft-times it is more irksome to let a small thing slip by than a large one, just as to do a small work rather than one which men would acclaim as great, may be a far greater effort.

In this way every man can go forward in the imitation of Christ as much as his shortcomings will allow it and yet need never feel far away from God.

May God help us.   Amen.

FINAL PRAYER

OH Lord and Father in Heaven: by thy eternal Love, which draws thee to mankind—I implore thee, bow down to me!

Oh Lord Jesus Christ: by the faithfulness with which thou accomplishest thy Work for the Honour and Praise of thy Father—I implore Thee, accomplish in me the praise due to Thy Father!

Oh Lord Jesus Christ: by the honour of thy Mother and the power of thy Death: I implore thee, destroy in me all ungodliness and implant thy Divine Countenance so that I may for ever praise Thee!

Amen.

* 9 7 8 1 6 6 6 7 7 7 1 5 4 *